Unmasking The Spectrum: Embracing the True Self and Shedding Light on the detrimental impact of Masking Autism.

By
Kim Silberman

Table of Contents

INTRODUCTION

In this heartfelt and enlightening book, you'll explore the challenges faced by individuals with autism and their families, while also delving into the triumphs and successes that come with embracing neurodiversity. Through real-life stories and expert insights, you'll gain a deep understanding of the unique perspectives and experiences of those living with autism. Unmasking Autism goes beyond stereotypes and confronts the stigma surrounding this condition. It offers practical strategies for overcoming barriers and fostering inclusive communities that celebrate individuality. From education and employment opportunities to self-advocacy and supportive networks, this book provides a comprehensive roadmap for empowering individuals with autism to reach their full potential. Whether you're a parent, caregiver, educator, or simply seeking a deeper understanding of autism, this book is your guide to unlocking solutions and promoting acceptance. Join the movement towards a more inclusive society, where individuals with autism are valued,

supported, and
celebrated for their
unique gifts and
contributions.
For every visibly
Autistic person you
meet, countless
"masked" Autistic
people pass as
neurotypical.
Masking is a
common coping
mechanism in which
Autistic people hide
their identifiable
Autistic traits in order
to fit in with societal
norms, adopting a
superficial
personality at the
expense of their
mental health. This
can include

suppressing harmless stimuli, papering over communication challenges by presenting as unassuming and mild-mannered, and forcing themselves into situations that cause severe anxiety, all so they aren't seen as needy or "odd."

Autism is a lifelong condition, but with appropriate support and interventions, individuals with autism can lead fulfilling lives and make valuable contributions to society. The focus of treatment and support is usually on addressing specific challenges, improving communication and social skills, and helping individuals with autism develop their strengths and abilities.

CHAPTER ONE:

1.1 WHAT IS AUTISM (Meaning of unmasking the spectrum)

Autism Spectrum Disorder (ASD) is a neurodevelopmental

condition
characterized by
distinct brain
differences. While
the precise causes
of ASD remain
complex, certain
individuals with ASD
exhibit identifiable
differences, including
those associated
with genetic
conditions.
Autism, also known
as Autism Spectrum
Disorder (ASD), is a
neurological disorder
that affects the way
a person perceives
and interacts with
the world. It is
characterized by
persistent challenges

in social communication and interaction, as well as restricted and repetitive patterns of behavior, interests, or activities.
The term "spectrum" in Autism Spectrum Disorder refers to the wide range of symptoms and severity levels that individuals with autism can experience. Some people with autism may have mild symptoms and be able to live independently, while others may have more significant

challenges that
require support and
assistance
throughout their
lives.
The exact cause of
autism is not yet fully
understood, but it is
believed to involve a
combination of
genetic and
environmental
factors. There is
currently no known
cure for autism, but
early intervention
and support can
greatly improve the
quality of life for
individuals with
autism.
Autism is typically
diagnosed in early

childhood, usually around the age of two or three, although it can sometimes be diagnosed earlier or later.

Recognizable Indicators and Symbols of Autism include:

Social communication difficulties: Challenges in understanding and using verbal and nonverbal communication, such as difficulty with maintaining eye contact, understanding

gestures, and
expressing
emotions.
Social interaction
challenges: Difficulty
with developing and
maintaining
relationships,
difficulty with social
interactions, and a
preference for
solitary activities.
Restricted and
repetitive behaviors:
Engaging in
repetitive
movements or
behaviors, such as
hand-flapping,
rocking, or repeating
words or phrases.
Individuals with
autism often show a

strong attachment to routines and may become upset with even small changes. Sensory sensitivities: Hypersensitivity to sensory stimuli, leading to discomfort or distress from loud noises, bright lights, certain textures, or strong smells. Hyposensitivity, where individuals may seek sensory stimulation, such as intense visual input or repetitive movements, to regulate sensory input.

Difficulty with
Transitions and
Changes:
Resistance to
changes in routines,
environments, or
plans, causing
distress or
meltdowns.
Challenges in
transitioning from
one activity to
another or adjusting
to new situations.

It is important to
note that each
person with autism is
unique, and the
symptoms they
experience can differ
greatly. While some
individuals with
autism may have

intellectual
disabilities, others
may possess
remarkable talents in
specific domains like
mathematics, music,
or visual arts.

1.2 MEANING OF MASKING.

Masking is a
prevalent coping
mechanism utilized
by individuals on the
autism spectrum, as
they strive to adapt
to a society
predominantly
oriented towards
neurotypical
behavior. Masking
entails various

behaviors, such as
consciously smiling
when deemed
socially acceptable,
diverting eye contact
by focusing between
the eyebrows to
alleviate discomfort
and suppressing
self-stimulatory
actions like hand
flapping, despite
finding them
comforting. It refers
to the act of
disguising specific
behaviors in order to
appear 'more normal'
to others, such as
feigning a smile or
simulating eye
contact by directing
one's gaze towards

the person's forehead." For certain individuals, constantly flapping their hands in public spaces serves as a soothing mechanism.

When I was young, I was diagnosed with autism. Sadly, I was born during a time when autism awareness was not widespread, which meant that I had to be mindful of how I appeared to others. My relatives would often ask me to refrain from certain movements, like fidgeting in the car or exhibiting certain behaviors at the dining table, as it made them feel uneasy. Back then, I wasn't fully aware that these actions were a form of self-stimulation.

Some reasons why individuals may engage in masking include a desire for social acceptance, avoidance of bullying or stigmatization, a need to maintain employment or relationships, or a lack of understanding and acceptance of autism within their environment. However, masking autism comes at a cost. The constant effort to mask one's true self can lead to increased stress, anxiety, mental health issues, and a sense of disconnection from one's own identity. It can also result in difficulties in self-advocacy, delayed diagnosis, and limited access to support and accommodations. In essence, Masking is very expensive. Living with autism, it's common to encounter remarks like "pay more attention to the topic," even though you're already fully engaged, despite your genuine focus, it might not appear that way to others, being neurotypical often leads to accusations of being inauthentic or "fake" when you're simply expressing yourself naturally. While it's true that many people occasionally adjust their behavior to fit into social norms, for individuals with

autism, the effort required to do so is often significantly heightened. The constant need to navigate social expectations can be exceptionally demanding and unsustainable in the long run.
Autistic individuals may sometimes feel that certain behaviors unique to them are shameful or disgusting, leading them to believe they need to hide from the world. However, these behaviors are often just coping

mechanisms utilized during sensory breakdowns, helping them manage overwhelming sensory experiences. Individuals with Autism from diverse backgrounds, including variations in race, color, or gender, employ different methods of masking. Consequently, those in their vicinity tend to assess them based on their unique historical background. Many individuals with autism often

receive the message
from a very young
age that they should
try to moderate their
behaviors,
particularly when
they exhibit
excessive
enthusiasm for their
interests, especially
if they have
undergone applied
behavior analysis
which is a
therapeutic approach
aimed at enhancing
targeted behaviors,
encompassing
various ideas
including social skills
communication,
reading, academics,
and adaptive

learning skills. These adaptive learning skills encompass fine motor dexterity, hygiene grooming, domestic capabilities, punctuality, and job competence.

2.1 AUTISM MASKING: Concealing or Modifying Symptoms (what it feels like to wear the mask).

There is a phenomenon known as "masking" within

the Autistic
Community, but it
extends beyond that
and applies to
various individuals
across different
diversity axes.
Masking involves the
efforts we make to
blend in with those
around us,
pretending to be
someone we're not -
less autistic, less
queer, less disabled,
less ADHD -
essentially, less of
ourselves.
Unfortunately, these
ideas are often
introduced or
reinforced through
behavioral methods

like ABA/IBI or
conversion therapy.
While masking might
provide temporary
relief by helping us
feel less strange or
different and making
others more
comfortable in our
presence, it poses
significant problems
for our mental well-
being as it strips
away our sense of
clear identity. Just as
actors/actresses
expend emotional
and physical energy
to portray characters
on screen or stage,
the energy required
to constantly pretend

to be someone we're not is substantial. The issue arises when, after a lifetime of masking, it isn't enough to simply "try harder" or "change our behavior" to mask less. At that point, we're essentially replacing one behavioral goal with another, without ever truly understanding who we are or experiencing the freedom that unmasking is meant to bring.

In the context of autism masking, individuals with

autism consciously or unconsciously develop coping mechanisms to hide or suppress their autistic traits in order to fit into social situations and appear more neurotypical. This masking can make it challenging to identify autism in these individuals.
 While it's important to note that experiences and symptoms can vary widely among people with autism, here are some common symptoms

associated with autism masking: Mimicking Social Behavior: Individuals may imitate the behavior of their neurotypical peers to blend in and appear socially adept. They might observe and copy facial expressions, body language, or speech patterns, even if they do not fully understand the underlying meaning or social cues. Mimicking Interests: Some individuals may adopt the interests or hobbies of others as a way to

connect with
neurotypical
individuals and
establish common
ground. They may
suppress or hide
their own intense
interests or
specialized
knowledge related to
specific topics, which
are characteristic of
autism.
Masking Sensory
Sensitivities: Many
individuals with
autism have sensory
sensitivities, such as
being overwhelmed
by certain sounds,
textures, or smells.
When masking, they
may suppress or

endure these sensitivities to avoid drawing attention to themselves or appearing different. Strategic Scripting: People who mask their autism often rely on pre-planned scripts or learned social responses to navigate social interactions. They may memorize appropriate conversational phrases or rehearse how to respond in different situations to seem more socially competent. Exhaustion and Burnout: Masking

requires significant effort and energy, leading to exhaustion and mental fatigue. Individuals may experience burnout due to continuously camouflaging their autistic traits, resulting in increased stress levels and potential mental health challenges.
Social Isolation: Despite the appearance of social skills, individuals who mask autism often struggle with forming authentic and meaningful

connections. They may feel isolated, as their true selves remain hidden, and maintaining social relationships becomes emotionally draining.

2.2 DETRIMENTS OF MASKING

This aims to explore the detrimental aspects of masking autism by examining various examples and providing evidence-based insights. By shedding light on the challenges faced by individuals who

mask their autism, we can foster a deeper understanding and advocate for a more inclusive and supportive society.
Emotional Toll: Masking autism takes a considerable emotional toll on individuals. The constant effort to camouflage one's true self can lead to increased stress, anxiety, and mental exhaustion. For example, an autistic individual may suppress their sensory sensitivities, such as noise

intolerance, in order to conform to social expectations. This suppression can lead to heightened anxiety and overwhelm, as they are constantly enduring uncomfortable situations without relief. Over time, this emotional burden can contribute to mental health issues and diminished overall well-being. Also, Autistic individuals often engage in self-stimulating behaviors, or stimming, as a way to regulate their sensory experiences and emotions. However, when masking, individuals may suppress stimming to avoid drawing attention to themselves. This suppression can lead to heightened anxiety and internal tension, as they are unable to release built-up stress effectively. The constant effort to hide stimming may also result in social exhaustion and emotional strain.

Social Isolation:

Masking autism can lead to a sense of social isolation. When individuals camouflage their autistic traits, they may struggle to find genuine connections and understanding from others. For instance, an autistic person who mimics social behaviors and conversations may find it challenging to establish meaningful relationships built on authentic communication. The fear of being exposed as different can result in a constant sense of

loneliness and a lack of genuine social interactions.
Misunderstanding and Lack of Support: By masking their autism, individuals often miss out on the understanding and support they deserve. When their struggles and needs are concealed, it becomes difficult for others to recognize and accommodate their unique challenges. For instance, an individual who camouflages their sensory sensitivities may not receive the

necessary accommodations, such as adjustments to lighting or noise levels, that could significantly improve their quality of life. The lack of support further perpetuates feelings of alienation and hampers their ability to thrive in various environments. Mental Health Implications: The impact of masking autism on mental health cannot be overstated. Autistic individuals who constantly mask their true selves are more susceptible to experiencing anxiety, depression, and burnout. For example, someone who exerts significant energy in scripting conversations to appear neurotypical may suffer from emotional exhaustion and increased levels of stress. The long-term consequences of such mental health challenges can hinder personal growth, academic or professional success, and overall life satisfaction.

Delayed Diagnosis and Treatment: Masking autism can also result in delayed diagnosis and appropriate treatment. When individuals effectively camouflage their autistic traits, it becomes more difficult for professionals to recognize the underlying condition. This delay in diagnosis can lead to missed opportunities for early intervention and tailored support, which are crucial for enhancing developmental outcomes. Without timely identification and interventions, individuals may face prolonged struggles and difficulties in various aspects of their lives.

Academic and professional challenges:

In educational and professional settings, masking autism can lead to significant challenges. Students or employees who mask may struggle to express their needs for accommodations, leading to increased stress and reduced performance. This lack of support may impede their academic and career growth, limiting their potential for success. Reduced Self-Advocacy: Masking can discourage individuals from advocating for their needs and rights. By constantly trying to blend in, they may hesitate to ask for accommodations or express their difficulties, which can limit their access to appropriate support and resources.

Masking autism may initially appear beneficial in terms of social conformity, but the long-term negative consequences cannot be ignored. The emotional toll, social isolation, lack of understanding and support, mental health implications, and delayed diagnosis and treatment all contribute to the harmful effects of masking. Society must promote acceptance, understanding, and support for individuals with autism, allowing them to embrace their authentic selves without fear of judgment or exclusion. By fostering an inclusive environment that celebrates neurodiversity, we can create a society that truly values and supports all individuals, regardless of their differences.

3.1 WHAT IS STIMMING?

Stimming, also known as self-stimulatory behavior, refers to repetitive or self-stimulating actions or behaviors that people engage in to regulate their sensory experiences or express their emotions. Stimming can involve a wide range of activities, including but not limited to:

refers to repetitive
or self-stimulating
actions or behaviors
that people engage
in to regulate their
sensory experiences
or express their
emotions. Stimming
can involve a wide
range of activities,
including but not
limited to:
Physical
movements:
Examples include
hand-flapping, body
rocking, spinning,
finger-waving, toe-
tapping, pacing, or
jumping. These
repetitive motions
can help individuals
with sensory

processing differences to manage sensory overload or provide a way to express excitement or anxiety.

Visual stimulation: Some individuals engage in repetitive visual behaviors, such as staring at moving objects, flicking their fingers in front of their eyes to observe the motion, or looking at lights or reflections. These activities may provide visual input that is soothing or stimulating for them.

Auditory stimulation: Stimming can involve making vocal sounds, such as humming, repeating words or phrases (echolalia), or producing certain sounds. These behaviors may serve as a means of self-soothing, self-expression, or sensory regulation. Tactile stimulation: Activities like rubbing or scratching surfaces, playing with textures, or repetitive touching can provide tactile stimulation that helps individuals regulate their sensory experiences or provide a sense of comfort.toe-tapping, pacing, or jumping. These repetitive motions can help individuals with sensory processing differences to manage sensory overload or provide a way to express excitement or anxiety.

Visual stimulation: Some individuals engage in repetitive visual behaviors, such as staring at moving objects, flicking their fingers in front of their eyes to observe the motion, or looking at lights or reflections. These activities may provide visual input that is soothing or stimulating for them. Auditory stimulation: Stimming can involve making vocal sounds, such as humming, repeating words or phrases (echolalia), or producing certain sounds. These behaviors may serve as a means of self-soothing, self-expression, or sensory regulation. Tactile stimulation: Activities like rubbing

or scratching
surfaces, playing
with textures, or
repetitive touching
can provide tactile
stimulation that helps
individuals regulate
their sensory
experiences or
provide a sense of
comfort.

3.2 MASKING VS STIMMING

Masking and
stimming are two
concepts often
associated with
neurodivergent
individuals,
particularly those on
the autism spectrum.

While there may be some overlapping behaviors or traits, there are several key differences between masking and stimming. Here are some of the differences:

Intention:

Masking: Masking is often intentional and driven by the desire to fit in or conform to social expectations.

Stimming: Stimming is typically unintentional and serves as a natural response to sensory experiences or emotional states.

Awareness:

Masking: Individuals who engage in masking are generally aware that they are suppressing their true selves or masking their neurodivergent traits. Stimming: People who stim may or may not be consciously aware of their stimming behaviors, as it often occurs instinctively. Social Conformity: Masking: Masking involves adapting one's behavior to conform to social norms and expectations, even if it requires

suppressing one's natural inclinations.
Stimming: Stimming behaviors are generally unrelated to social conformity and are more focused on self-regulation or self-expression.
External Perception:
Masking: Masking often aims to present oneself as neurotypical to others, concealing neurodivergent traits or behaviors.
Stimming: Stimming behaviors can be noticeable to others and may be interpreted as

unusual or atypical,
depending on the
context.
Emotional Impact:
Masking: Masking
can have a
significant emotional
impact, as
individuals may
experience feelings
of exhaustion,
frustration, or even a
loss of identity from
constantly
suppressing their
true selves.
Stimming: Stimming
is often a way for
individuals to
regulate their
emotions, reduce
anxiety, or find
comfort, providing a

positive emotional impact.
Voluntary vs. Involuntary:
Masking: Masking is a voluntary action undertaken by the individual to adapt to their environment and social expectations.
Stimming: Stimming is often an involuntary or spontaneous response to internal or external stimuli, serving as a coping mechanism.
Repetitiveness:
Masking: Masking behaviors are typically not

repetitive but involve modifying or suppressing certain aspects of behavior or expression.
Stimming: Stimming behaviors are characterized by their repetitive nature, involving actions such as hand-flapping, rocking, or repeating phrases.
Sensory Focus:
Masking: Masking primarily focuses on behavioral and social aspects, such as modifying speech patterns, body language, or facial expressions.

Stimming: Stimming often revolves around sensory experiences and aims to provide sensory regulation, such as by seeking tactile, auditory, or visual stimulation. Coping mechanism: Masking: Masking is a coping mechanism employed to navigate social environments and avoid potential stigma or discrimination. Stimming: Stimming is also a coping mechanism, but it primarily serves to regulate sensory input or manage emotional states rather than social interaction.

It's important to note that these differences are not mutually exclusive, and individuals may engage in both masking and stimming behaviors to varying degrees. The experiences and manifestations of masking and stimming can differ across individuals within the neurodivergent community.

4.1 WHAT EXACTLY IS UNMASKING THE SPECTRUM?

The process of openly expressing one's authentic self as an autistic individual refers to as "Unmasking". Ceasing to engage in camouflaging behaviors often brings immense relief to autistic individuals. It refers to the process of shedding the metaphorical mask

that individuals with autism often wear to blend in with neurotypical society. It involves breaking free from the camouflage and allowing one's true colors to shine through.
Unmasking holds immense importance for autistic individuals. By embracing their authentic selves, they can experience a profound sense of relief and acceptance. Unmasking allows them to fully embrace their

strengths, passions, and unique perspectives, which are often overshadowed or overlooked when they are camouflaging. Furthermore, unmasking fosters self-advocacy, empowerment, and the development of a strong autistic identity. It encourages autistic individuals to assert their needs, advocate for inclusive environments, and challenge societal misconceptions

about autism.
Unmasking has the potential to bring about significant positive changes in the lives of autistic individuals. By embracing their authentic selves, they can experience improved mental health, reduced stress, and increased self-esteem. Unmasking also paves the way for meaningful connections and relationships based on genuine understanding and acceptance. Additionally,

unmasking allows autistic individuals to contribute their unique perspectives and talents to society, promoting diversity, innovation, and inclusivity. Unmasking autism, therefore, focuses on encouraging individuals with autism to express their authentic selves and promoting acceptance of their autistic traits. It aims to create an environment where individuals feel comfortable and supported in being their true selves, rather than feeling the need to constantly mask or hide their autistic characteristics.

4.2 UNMASKING THROUGH A VALUE-BASED INTEGRATION EXERCISE

In today's diverse and interconnected world, understanding and embracing different perspectives and values is crucial for fostering genuine connections and building harmonious relationships.

Unmasking, a
process of
uncovering and
exploring one's true
self, can be a
transformative
journey that leads to
personal growth and
improved
interpersonal
dynamics. To
embark on this
journey, a values-
based integration
exercise provides an
effective framework.
This exercise
enables individuals
to delve into their
core values,
examine the masks
they wear in different
contexts, and

ultimately align their actions with their authentic selves. By following the steps outlined in this guide, individuals can embark on a path of self-discovery and cultivate more meaningful connections with others. Let's delve into the essential steps of unmasking through a values-based integration exercise and explore the profound impact it can have on personal and interpersonal development.

•Reflect on five significant moments in your life where you felt truly alive, spanning from childhood to adulthood, encompassing various aspects such as school, work, vacations, or hobbies. These moments might have evoked a sense of satisfaction or fulfillment. Capture each of these experiences on individual pages within a notebook or document on your device.

•The next step is to get as much information as you can about these moments. Think explicitly about WHY this particular moment has affected you so profoundly. Give as many specifics as you can while retelling the event's account.
•After you've completed telling each of your five stories, go back over and look for keywords that define each one. Most stories will include at least two or three key terms and some

important words will
be repeated_ this is
typical.
•Make a list of all the
keywords on a
separate page. Many
people will discover
that they have 10-20
terms on this list.
More or less than
that is OK, but you
should have at least
5-6.
•Consider your list
again. How do these
words make you
feel? Do they all feel
important? Are there
any terms that are
very essential to you
that you are
missing? (Be
cautious not to add

phrases you merely THINK are important- attempt to tie them back to a moment when you felt Alive if they don't fit, leave them out).
•If you have more than 5-6 words, consider whether some of them appear to clump together.
•Try rearranging and shuffling the words until they appear to fit into no more than 5-6 groupings in total.
•Try to find a single term that summarizes the notion for you using

your words or word groupings. Then, clarify what each of these words means to you.

•It might be beneficial to incorporate as many of the terms from your groups as possible into your definition in order to capture all of the notions you've identified.

Unmasking autism involves several aspects:

Awareness: Increasing awareness and understanding of autism among the

general population to
promote acceptance
and reduce stigma
surrounding the
condition.
Self-advocacy:
Encouraging
individuals with
autism to advocate
for themselves,
express their needs,
and seek appropriate
support and
accommodations.
Supportive
environments:
Creating inclusive
and accommodating
environments that
respect and embrace
neurodiversity,
enabling individuals
with autism to feel

comfortable expressing themselves authentically. Sensory considerations: Recognizing and addressing sensory sensitivities that individuals with autism may experience, such as sensitivity to loud noises or certain textures, and providing appropriate accommodations. Foster open communication: Encourage open and honest communication. Create opportunities

for autistic
individuals to share
their thoughts,
feelings, and
experiences without
judgment or
criticism. Listen
actively and respect
their perspectives.
Celebrate strengths
and interests:
Recognize and
celebrate the unique
strengths, talents,
and interests of
autistic individuals.
Encourage them to
pursue their
passions and
provide opportunities
for them to
showcase their
abilities.

Collaborate with professionals: Work collaboratively with professionals, such as educators, therapists, and support providers, who have experience in supporting autistic individuals.
 Mindfulness and Stress Management: Incorporate stress-reducing techniques into your routine, such as deep breathing exercises, meditation, yoga, or engaging in hobbies and interests that promote relaxation.

They can provide
guidance, strategies,
and resources to
support the
unmasking process.
By unmasking
autism, society can
foster a more
inclusive and
understanding
culture that values
and appreciates the
diverse experiences
and perspectives of
individuals on the
autism spectrum.

CONCLUSION

Unmasking the
Spectrum has been
a journey of
discovery, empathy,

and hope. Throughout this book, we have delved into the intricate world of autism, exploring its many facets, unraveling its complexities, and shedding light on the experiences of individuals living with this condition. We have challenged misconceptions, shattered stereotypes, and opened our minds and hearts to a more profound understanding of autism.

We have learned
that autism is not a
monolithic entity but
a vast spectrum of
unique perspectives,
abilities, and
challenges. It is a
neurodevelopmental
condition that
manifests differently
in each person,
encompassing a
wide range of
strengths, talents,
and interests. By
unmasking autism,
we have lifted the
veil that obscures
the true potential and
brilliance of those on
the spectrum.
Throughout this
journey, we have

emphasized the importance of acceptance, inclusion, and support. We have recognized that a society that embraces diversity and fosters understanding is one where individuals with autism can thrive. It is crucial to provide the necessary resources, educational opportunities, and employment options to enable individuals on the spectrum to reach their full potential and lead fulfilling lives. Moreover, we have highlighted the significance of early intervention and the power of therapeutic approaches tailored to the unique needs of individuals with autism. By recognizing and addressing challenges early on, we can enhance communication, social skills, and overall quality of life for those affected by this condition.

It is essential to remember that unmasking autism is

not solely the responsibility of individuals on the spectrum or their families. It is a collective effort that involves communities, educators, healthcare professionals, policymakers, and society at large. By working together, we can create a world that not only accepts autism but also celebrates the diversity and contributions of those living with this condition.

As we bring this journey to a close, let us carry forward the knowledge gained from "Unmasking Autism" and advocate for a more inclusive and compassionate world. Let us embrace differences, challenge stereotypes, and foster an environment where every individual, regardless of their neurological makeup, can live a life of dignity, purpose, and fulfillment.

By unmasking
autism, we have
embarked on a
transformative path,
one that offers hope,
understanding, and a
brighter future for all.
Let us continue to
walk this path with
empathy, respect,
and a commitment to
creating a world
where every voice is
heard and every life
is valued.